THE LAST
TRUMPET

THE LAST TRUMPET

HOPE FOR THE TRIBULATION SAINTS

NELSON A. CAMPOS

iUniverse LLC
Bloomington

THE LAST TRUMPET
HOPE FOR THE TRIBULATION SAINTS

iUniverse books may be ordered through booksellers or by contacting:

iUniverse LLC
1663 Liberty Drive
Bloomington, IN 47403
www.iuniverse.com
1-800-Authors (1-800-288-4677)

Because of the dynamic nature of the Internet, any web addresses or
links contained in this book may have changed since publication and
may no longer be valid. The views expressed in this work are solely those
of the author and do not necessarily reflect the views of the publisher,
and the publisher hereby disclaims any responsibility for them.

Any people depicted in stock imagery provided by Thinkstock are models,
and such images are being used for illustrative purposes only.
Certain stock imagery © Thinkstock.

ISBN: 978-1-4917-2456-9 (sc)
ISBN: 978-1-4917-2457-6 (e)

Library of Congress Control Number: 2014902187

Printed in the United States of America.

iUniverse rev. date: 04/30/2014

Unless otherwise indicated, all scripture references
are from the ~ King James Version ~
~ KJV ~

Cover Image by: Richard Campos . . . The Pelican Nebula.

CONTENTS

Dedicated to my wife, Eve;
our three children: Richard, Lisa, and Rachelle;
and our three grandchildren: Kyle, Jamie, and Robert.

PREFACE

Being blessed with the opportunity to listen to Christian radio over the years, I was able to receive an abundance of teachings regarding biblical content, application, and prophecy. These teachings came primarily from prominent biblical scholars, such as Dr. J. Vernon McGee, Dr. Charles Stanley, Dr. David Hocking, Gary Stearman, Chuck Missler, and a host of others, including Hal Lindsey, Chuck Smith, and Chuck Swindle.

Listeners seek their guidance to provide a basic understanding of scriptural matters; but, inevitably, there comes a time in our learning when we find ourselves beginning to question certain teaching.

A lack of confidence in our ability to understand and study scriptures on our own may cause us to blindly follow certain traditional teachings. However, there are an abundance of Bible tools available to anyone who desires to learn without relying fully on the insights of others.

After listening to many teachings and commentaries, we can naturally develop our own understanding of certain biblical subjects. Hopefully this comes with the help and guidance of the Holy Spirit.

I personally enjoy the study of Bible prophecy in light of the times and current world events. And boy, are they exciting.

Anyone who studies biblical prophecy—especially in regard to how it relates to future events—can become frustrated over the controversy surrounding the rapture of the church, particularly in relationship to the future seven-year tribulation period. There never seems to be a clear-cut argument or resolution that would prove to be the correct interpretation while, at the same time, clearly disproving other views.

After hearing the arguments for and against each view, some students of prophecy may lean toward the pretribulation view. This is what I have done, mainly because I feel the evidence for this view is more convincing. After reaching this point, I set aside any further concern for this subject for several years.

One night while watching the Praise the Lord program on the Trinity Broadcasting Network (TBN), something caught my attention. Paul and Jan Crouch were cohosts for that evening. Their special guest was Joseph Good with Hatikva Ministries in Port Arthur, Texas.

I was fascinated with Mr. Good's teaching on Rosh Hashanah (the Jewish New Year). At one point during the teaching, Paul Crouch asked Mr. Good how the tribulation saints ended up being in heaven with the Lord. I really appreciated Mr. Good's answer. It was an honest one. He admitted that he didn't have a theory on that and that he just didn't know.

Ever since, that same question has been nagging me. Approximately five years later, I decided to do a study on the matter. I got to wondering, if I was left behind after the rapture of the church and came to acknowledge and receive the Lord Jesus as my savior during the tribulation, what would be my hope of escape from such a terrible time? Would I be able to survive for seven years until the coming of the Lord, or would I be killed for my faith? What would be my hope of escape from persecution or death?

During the tribulation, millions will come to the shocking realization of what has happened; many will turn to the Lord. I suspect they will be looking for a way to escape, just as I am looking for the Lord to get me out of this messed-up world before it turns completely evil.

I have begun to look at scriptures a little differently, with more concern and increased sensitivity toward the tribulation saints. It's been about twenty years since I began toying with this question. At this time, I feel I may have something to offer—something that might stimulate others to further consider the plight of the tribulation saint.

Hindsight tends to be more accurate than foresight. Those who hold to a dogmatic view of certain future events may find themselves rather humbled when future events finally unfold.

The Word of God will be just as valid for those on the other side of the rapture during the seven-year tribulation period as it is on this side of the rapture. Those who find themselves in the tribulation period will have the advantage of hindsight when interpreting scripture.

I will be presenting some questions to those who hold fast to particular views and to those who refuse to accept the possibility of other views having some validity. My aim is not to disprove any particular view, but I hope to reconcile and bring into harmony opposing views. Here are the three most common views of the rapture:

1. The rapture will take place prior to the start of the tribulation period.

2. The rapture will take place during the middle of the tribulation.
3. The rapture will take place near the end of the tribulation.

From this point on, because of my understanding of the rapture, I often used the word translation in lieu of the word rapture. I hope to make it clear why I chose to do so as we progress further into this book.

Let us see if we can bring these views into harmony. If so, then everybody can claim a part of this controversial pie. But more important is to bring fourth truth so that all may learn and be strengthened in hope, especially those who will have to endure and survive during the tribulation period until the coming of the Lord.

My hope is to persuade the church-age saints and, at the same time, give assurance to the tribulation saints regarding the possibility of multiple events of the same nature, when living believers in Christ will be translated, caught up, or gathered into the presence of the Lord in the heavens.

The first event will take place before the start of the seven-year tribulation period, when the dead in Christ rise, as stated in 1 Thessalonians 4:16, "*and the dead in Christ shall rise first.*"

The second event will take place in the middle of the tribulation, when the man child is caught up to God and his throne in Revelation 12:5: "*And she brought forth a man child, who was to rule all nations with a rod of iron: and her child was caught up unto God, and to his throne.*"

A third event will occur at the end of the tribulation period, when the saints who are alive and survive the seven-year tribulation period will then be gathered together, as Jesus stated in Matthew 24:31—"*And he shall send his angels with a great sound of a trumpet, and they shall gather together his elect from the four winds, from one end of heaven to the other"*—and as John stated in Revelation 14:16—*"And he that sat on the cloud thrust in his sickle on the earth; and the earth was reaped."*

There will be a final gathering of the gentile nations. This will be a nonrapture event. They will be gathered for judgment at the end of the tribulation period, as stated in Matthew 25:33-34, 41: *"And he shall set the sheep on his right hand, but the goats on the left. Then shall the King say unto them on his right hand, Come, ye blessed of my Father, inherit the kingdom prepared for you from the foundation of the world . . . Then shall he say also unto them on the left hand, Depart from me, ye cursed, into everlasting fire, prepared for the devil and his angels."*

The gentile nations are symbolized as being a goat nation or a sheep nation. The goat nations are cast into everlasting fire, and the sheep nations are allowed to inherit the earthly kingdom during the millennium.

I hope to present some questions that are challenging and will strike your curiosity. So if you'll just hang on for a while; you just might find this interesting.

As a student of Bible prophecy, I am attempting to communicate my own personal understanding of scripture. I do so with reliance upon the Holy Spirit for his guidance and insight.

Scriptural instruction allows us to communicate our thoughts, ideas, and understanding of the Word of God:

> *Let the prophets speak two or three, and let the others judge . . . For ye may all prophesy one by one, that all may learn, and all may be comforted.*
> (1 Corinthians 14:29, 31)

> *Knowing this first, that no prophecy of scripture is of
> any private interpretation.* (2 Peter 1:20)

My understanding of 1 Corinthians 4:29-33 and 2 Peter 1:20-21 is simple and without confusion.

1. No one person has full insight into all the scriptures. God gives much insight to a few of his prominent servants, such as those who penned the Word of God and to our present-day prophets and spiritual leaders. I believe he also gives understanding and insight to each of his servants, whether they are of prominence or not, according to his will and purpose.

2. You cannot take any one scripture and build a scenario with it. Truth is found when the whole counsel of God (the Word) is applied.

Knowing God is not a respecter of persons, I believe the insight given to the multitudes of his servants and its accumulative importance is in every way as valuable as is the insight given to the prominent few.

Since we know that God is not the author of confusion, we must then conclude confusion comes from the devil himself and is manifested through the pride of man.

If we want to unconfuse the works of Satan, let us try to reconcile and seek the harmony of the scriptures.

CHAPTER 1

So, What's the Problem?

We, the living church-age saints who are on this side of the pretribulation translation (commonly called rapture), tend to interpret future events as though we have all the insight necessary to be conclusive in our views.

This is often the case when we look at the treatment of 1 Thessalonians 4:13-18. It seems like every time I hear someone teach or, in an excitable way, talk about the pretribulation translation, they only quote verses 16 and 17: *"For the Lord himself shall descend from heaven with a shout, with the voice of the archangel, and with the trump of God: and the dead in Christ shall rise first: Then we which are alive and remain shall be caught up together with them in the clouds, to meet the Lord in the air: and so shall we ever be with the Lord."*

I get excited when I think about the Lord's soon return and our being taken out of this world and into his presence. However, when these two verses are quoted in this manner, it tends to misdirect the emphasis that the apostle Paul was placing in verse 18: *"Wherefore comfort one another with these words."*

I get a little upset when this happens, because focusing on verses 16-17 does not bring out the true meaning of the passage. I believe that Paul's intention was for all the words in the passage, from verses 13 through 18, to be a comfort to the reader—both to the pretribulation and the tribulation saint.

Just what group of saints does this passage (1 Thessalonians 4:13-18) pertain to? Is it the church-age saints or the tribulation saints? Or could it be both groups?

If it is meant to comfort the church-age saints only, then as soon as the pretribulation translation takes place and the dead in Christ rise first, this passage will no longer apply to the tribulation saints. The tribulation saints would have to interpret this passage as a prophecy already fulfilled.

They would have to conclude that the Lord has already descended from heaven with a shout, with the voice of the archangel, and with the trump of God. Those believers who were alive and remained would already be caught up to meet the Lord in the air with the dead in Christ who rose first.

However, we know that the Lord descends to earth at the end of the tribulation and not before, as was foretold by the word of the Lord in Matthew 24:29, 31: "*Immediately after the tribulation of those days shall the sun shall be darkened, and the moon shall not give her light, and the stars shall fall from heaven, and the powers of the heavens shall be shaken . . . And he shall send his angels with a great sound of a trumpet, and they shall gather together his elect from the four winds, from one end of heaven to the other.*"

If this passage is also valid for the tribulation saints, we now have another problem. For example, one would have to conclude that those who are alive and remain are those who did not get translated to heaven when the dead in Christ, all living believers, rose first. From their point of view, Christ has not yet returned to the earth and the catching away, the rapture, is still to come. Do you see the problem?

So what does it mean to remain? The answer to this can be found in 1 Thessalonians 4:15, 17: *"For this we say unto you by the word of the Lord, that we which are alive and remain unto the coming of the Lord shall not prevent them which are asleep . . . Then we which are alive and remain* [unto the coming of the Lord] *shall be caught up together with them in the clouds, to meet the Lord in the air: and so shall we ever be with the Lord."*

Please note: In verse 17, I inserted in brackets the words Paul used in verse 15. I feel this best describes those who are left behind to survive until the coming of the Lord when he gathers his elect at the end of the tribulation period; as described by Jesus in Matthew 24:31: *"And he shall send his angels with a great sound of a trumpet, and they shall gather together his elect from the four winds, from one end of heaven to the other."*

The Strong's Concordance defines the word remain as "to *survive."* Based on this definition, the verse should read, *"we who are alive and survive until the coming of the Lord."*

What could possibly bring about a condition that would thereby force the pretribulation believers into a state of survival, especially if there is only a brief interval between the time the dead in Christ rise first and those who are alive and remain are caught up with them? If there is only a second, a minute, or an hour, what is so unique to those who are alive and remain that would not have been unique to all the saints since Pentecost or even to nonbelievers during that particular event?

It just isn't logical to try to apply the definition of the word survive to the pretribulation saints when it best describes those saints during the tribulation who must survive until the coming of the Lord, as described in 1 Thessalonians 4:15: *"For this we say unto you by the word of the Lord, that we which are alive and remain unto the coming of the Lord shall not prevent them which are asleep."*

I believe the survival state for those who are left behind during the tribulation period will be brought about by the disappearance of the millions of people who were taken out of this world to be with the Lord. This event will be closely followed by a time of confusion and the realization that those who remain will be persecuted, even unto death, if they choose to accept and follow the Lord Jesus during the tribulation period.

Vine's Complete Expository Dictionary states that the word remain, as it is used in 1 Thessalonians 4:15-17, refers to the living believers at the time of the Lords physical return, arrival, and presence.

If this is so, then I conclude that those who are still alive and remain and survive until the coming of the Lord at the end of the tribulation period will have the hope of being caught up or raptured alive before they are killed for their faith. The rapture will become the hope of the living and surviving tribulation saints.

There are two groups of living believers spoken of in 1 Thessalonians 4:16-17: *"For the Lord himself shall descend from heaven with a shout, with the voice of the archangel, and with the trump of God: and the dead in Christ shall rise first: Then we which are alive and remain shall be caught up together with them in the clouds, to meet the Lord in the air: and so shall we ever be with the Lord."*

The first group consists of the dead in Christ who rise first. This group includes only the living believers who are alive when the pretribulation translation occurs.

The second group consists of those saints who are left behind and survive the tribulation period until the coming of the Lord. This second group also includes only living believers.

The reason I do not include the saints who are asleep in the grave, whether or not they died before or during the tribulation period, is because of the implications of the apostle Paul's words in 2 Corinthians 5:6, 8: "*Therefore we are always confident, knowing that, whilst we are at home in the body, we are absent from the Lord . . . we are confident, I say, and willing rather to be absent from the body, and to be present with the Lord.*"

When a person dies the body goes in the grave. Being corruptible, the body decays and returns to the dust. That which goes immediately to be with the Lord is a person's spirit.

CHAPTER 2

Who Are the Dead in Christ Who Rise First?

If we accept the possibility that those who are alive and remain until the coming of the Lord are the tribulation saints, then who are the dead in Christ who rise first?

General consensus is that the dead in Christ who rise first at the pretribulation translation event are only the church-age saints who have physically died and are asleep in the grave. And then, almost immediately after this event, the living saints will be translated to heaven with them. The two translations are usually considered to be the one pretribulation rapture event.

Now, I am going to ask you, the reader, to cut me a little slack regarding my understanding of who the dead in Christ are. I'm going to take the same liberty as highly respected Bible teachers and scholars (such as Dr. J. Vernon McGee, Hal Lindsey, Dr. Charles Stanley, and others) have taken in the past and suggest that maybe a particular Greek word might be better translated differently.

My understanding is that the group of believers mentioned in 1 Thessalonians 4:16-*"and the dead in Christ shall rise first"*—who get translated to heaven consists only of living believers. I hope to make clear why I believe as I do as we continue.

Let's begin with the apostle Paul and his use of the word dead. I would like to persuade you that when Paul spoke of the dead in Christ rising first, he was speaking only of living believers who are alive during the pretribulation translation event.

We can get an idea of how Paul uses the word dead in Romans 6:2, 7-8, 11 when read in context of the passage. *"God forbid. How shall we, that are dead to sin, live any longer therein? . . . For he that is dead is freed from sin. Now if we be dead with Christ, we believe that we shall also live with him . . . Likewise reckon ye also yourselves to be dead unto sin, but alive unto God through Jesus Christ our Lord."*

Note: My NKJ shorthand version of verse 11 is *"reckon yourselves to be dead in Christ."*

When the restrainer, the Holy Spirit, is taken out of the way as in 2 Thessalonians 2:7: *"For the mystery of iniquity doth already work: only he who now letteth will let, until he be taken out of the way,"* then the dead in Christ, the living believers, will be translated; rising first into heaven.

This is the event that will allow the Antichrist to be revealed, thus setting the stage for the tribulation period to commence.

Paul's message is to living believers. Though he is speaking to them as if they are dead, he is describing a spiritual condition in reference to sin. Sin is a rebellious nature toward God and a rejection of the things of God.

When the spirit is physically separated from the body, the body is dead. *"For as the body without the spirit is dead"* (James 2:26).

As the spirit is separated from the corruptible flesh, we should separate ourselves spiritually from corruptible sin.

Paul is also speaking of a spiritual condition of being alive and in Christ. One becomes spiritually alive and in Christ when one trusts in God's plan and work of salvation. This work of salvation was performed by his unique son at a place called Calvary, over two thousand years ago.

I believe a pretribulation translation occurs when the dead in Christ—that is, the living believers—rise first, as spoken of in 1 Thessalonians 4:16, *"and the dead in Christ shall rise first."*

Then those who are left behind and receive Christ during the tribulation period will have to remain alive and survive until the coming of the Lord at the end of the tribulation. It's at that time that the surviving saints will be caught up to meet the Lord when he gathers his elect.

It is my opinion that in Romans 6:11 Paul is speaking of the living church-age saints who have died to sin spiritually; and are spiritually alive in Christ: *"Likewise reckon ye also yourselves to be dead indeed unto sin, but alive unto God through Jesus Christ our Lord."*

CHAPTER 3

The Restrainer

Most Bible teachers agree that "he who now letteth," the restrainer, is the Holy Spirit of God who indwells those who have received Jesus as their Messiah. This occurs when one becomes born-again of the spirit of God, as spoken of by Jesus in John 3:3: *"Jesus answered and said unto him, Verily, verily, I say unto thee, Except a man be <u>born again</u>, he cannot see the kingdom of God."*

When the restrainer, the indwelling Holy Spirit, is taken out of the way, the church-age saints, the body of Christ, will be taken out with him. I believe this to be true because of the promise Jesus made in John 14:3, 17: *"And if I go and prepare a place for you, I will come again, and receive you unto myself; that where I am, there ye may be also . . . Even the Spirit of truth; whom the world cannot receive, because it seeth him not, neither knoweth him: but ye know him; for he dwelleth with you, and shall be in you."*

Jesus said he would not leave us comfortless. He said he would have to go and prepare a place for us in his father's house and he would ask the father to send us a comforter, one who will guide us into all truth and understanding. He also promised that the comforter, the Holy Spirit, would dwell in us and be with us forever.

We need to let this sink in. Forever means forever and forever. Get the idea? So when you become born-again, you are indwelled with and sealed with the Holy Spirit forever.

I take comfort in knowing that when the restrainer is taken out of the way, the Holy Spirit will not abandon the church-age saints. After the Holy Spirit is taken out of the way along with the church-age saints, Jesus will come again and receive the tribulation saints unto himself. He will catch them up, and they will meet him and be with him in the heavens forever.

With the restrainer and the church-age saints gone, it makes it possible for the Antichrist to be revealed and unrestrained. And then the seven-year tribulation will begin, according to God's will and timing. At that time, God will still be pouring out his spirit upon those who are left behind and upon those who survive until the coming of the Lord.

The coming of Jesus will be at the end of the final seventh year of Daniel's seventieth week of years. It is then that the Lord will gather his elect, during the Feast of Trumpets.

This will be the final Last Trumpet of the dispensational age of grace. It will be the fulfillment of Leviticus 23:23-24, according to God's appointed time: "*And the Lord spake unto Moses, saying, Speak unto the children of Israel, saying, In the seventh month, in the first day of the month, shall ye have a sabbath, a memorial of blowing of trumpets, an holy convocation.*"

Just because the indwelling Holy Spirit and the church-age saints are gone, that doesn't mean the Holy Spirit is not at work. It is still the grace of God that will bring salvation during the tribulation period. The tribulation believer will still be saved by God's grace through their faith in the Lord Jesus.

CHAPTER 4

The Catching Away of the Man Child

I hope this will prove to be a most interesting chapter. I am going to lay out an interpretation that perhaps may cause you to rethink who or what the "man child" is in reference to Revelation 12:5. I hope this interpretation will pique your curiosity and cause you to give further consideration as to who the man child is or is not.

The most popular view of Revelation 12:5 is that the man child is the Lord Jesus: *"And she brought forth a man child, who was to rule all nations with a rod of iron: and her child was caught up unto God, and to his throne."*

When I first started studying the Bible, I had to rely on others to at least put me in the ballpark when trying to understand the book of Revelation.

My favorite Bible commentator was the highly respected Dr. James Vernon McGee with his Through the Bible radio program. Dr. McGee interprets the man child to be the Lord Jesus. Anyone who holds the same view as Dr. McGee stands in great company.

I believe this popular interpretation comes out of several passages. The first passage to reference is Psalm 2:6, 9 with the emphasis being on verses 9: "*Yet have I set my king upon my holy hill of Zion . . . Thou shalt break them with a rod of iron; thou shalt dash them in pieces like a potter's vessel.*" I accept these verses as making reference to the Lord Jesus.

The second passage to reference is Revelation 19:15-16: "*And out of his mouth goeth a sharp sword, that with it he should smite the nations: and he shall rule them with a rod of iron: and he treadeth the winepress of the fierceness and wrath of Almighty God. And he hath on his vesture and on his thigh a name written, KING OF KINGS, AND LORD OF LORDS.*"

The Lord comes out of heaven on a white horse, and the armies of heaven are with him. In verse 15, he demonstrates his authority. In verse 16, he is identified as the King of Kings and Lord of Lords. I also accept this passage as making reference to our Lord Jesus.

Now, if I believe that Revelation 19:15-16 is speaking of the Lord Jesus and how he is to rule the nations with a rod of iron, how can I possibly believe that the man child in Revelation 12:5 is *not* the Lord Jesus? "*And she brought forth a man child, who was to rule all nations with a rod of iron: and her child was caught up unto God, and to his throne.*"

Psalm 2:6-9, and Revelation 19:15-16 both speak of the lord Jesus, however I found reason to believe that the man child of Revelation 12:5 is not the Lord.

At this point I want to redirect your thinking. While studying Revelation 12:5, I found several reasons to rethink my view of the man child.

<u>First Reason:</u> *Others* will also rule the nations with a rod of iron.

<u>Second Reason</u>: The *time frame* in which the man child is caught up does not match up with the time of Jesus ascension.

<u>Third Reason</u>: The man child is *caught up.*

The *first* reason I found is in Revelation 2:26-27: *"And he that overcometh, and keepeth my works unto the end, to him will I give power over nations: And he shall rule them with a rod of iron; as the vessels of a potter shall they be broken to shivers: even as I received of my Father."*

These verses in Revelation 2:26-27 are in reference to Psalm 2:8-9. It is restated by Jesus himself when he was giving instructions to John as to what to write to the church in Thyatira.

In verses 24-27 Jesus makes a promise to those who overcometh and keeps his works until the end. Jesus says he will give them authority over the nations, just as he received from his Father. Then Jesus goes on and restates Psalm 2:9.

Because of the promise Jesus made in Revelation 2:26-27; I believe there are others who will also rule the nations with a rod of iron.

The *second* reason stems from the Apostle John's account of the time frame during which the man child is caught up.

I have heard it said that the Ten Commandments are not the ten suggestions, recommendations, or requests; they are commandments. To put it military lingo, if the Lord commands you to jump, on your way up you ask, "How high, Lord?" Jesus said in John 14:15, *"If ye love me, keep my commandments."*

Now, I am hard-pressed to believe that the apostle John would not be obedient to the Lords every command.

In Revelation 1:11, Jesus commanded John, "*What thou seest, write in a book, and send it unto the seven churches which are in Asia.*"

Jesus again commands John to write what he has seen, the things that are, and what will take place in the future: "*Write the things which thou hast seen, and the things which are, and the things which shall be hereafter*" (In Revelation 1:19).

In Revelation chapters 2 and 3, John again is obedient to the Lord and writes of the things that are—that is, the conditions of the seven churches in Asia, including their favorable and unfavorable points.

I ask you these questions: When the Lord commanded John to write about the things that were to take place after he wrote about the things that are, did John obey the Lord? Did he write about the things that were to take place in his future? I don't think there is any doubt. John wrote what he was commanded to write and in the correct order.

We know the Lord was born in the year AD 1. We also know he was taken up to heaven in a cloud at his ascension, approximately in AD 33. According to the time line given in the NKJV Open Bible, John wrote the book approximately sixty-three years later, sometime around AD 95-96.

What John writes about in chapter 4 and beyond must take place in John's future, which is after AD 95-96.

Everything John writes about from Revelation 4:1 and beyond John saw while in the spirit; those things he saw will take place in his future. "*After this I looked, and, behold, a door was opened in heaven: and the first voice which I heard was as it were of a trumpet talking with me; which said, Come up hither, and I will shew thee things which must be hereafter*" (Revelation 4:1).

Keep in mind that Jesus was taken up to heaven in John's past, before he wrote the book of Revelation.

The man child of Revelation 12:5 will be caught up after John writes the book of Revelation.

The time frame in which the man child is caught up is commonly thought to be in the middle of the seven-year tribulation period. This is when the devil is cast out of heaven and down to earth as stated in Revelation 12:13: *"And when the dragon saw that he was cast unto the earth, he persecuted the woman which brought forth the man child"*.

It is also the time the abomination of desolation takes place, as spoken of by Jesus in Matthew 24:15: *"When ye therefore shall see the abomination of desolation, spoken of by Daniel the prophet, stand in the holy place, (whoso readeth, let him understand)."*

In Daniel 9:27, in the middle of the week is when the Antichrist sets up the abomination of desolation causing the *Great* tribulation to begin.

The following passage is commonly thought to be the event that starts the seven-year tribulation period: *"And he shall confirm the covenant with many for one week: and in the midst of the week he shall cause the sacrifice and the oblation to cease, and for the overspreading of abominations he shall make it desolate, even until the consummation, and that determined shall be poured upon the desolate"* (Daniel 9:27).

In Matthew 24:16, Jesus gave a warning to those in Jerusalem who would see the abomination of desolation spoken of by the prophet Daniel: *"Then let them which be in Judaea flee into the mountains."*

Let us now consider the woman in Revelation 12:1-2, 5, 13-14. The woman is generally thought to be the symbol of the nation of Israel.

And there appeared a great wonder in heaven; a woman clothed with the sun, and the moon under her feet, and upon her head a crown of twelve stars: And she being with child cried, travailing in birth, and pained to be delivered . . . And she brought forth a man child, who was to rule all nations with a rod of iron: and her child was caught up unto God, and to his throne . . . And when the dragon saw that he was cast unto the earth, he persecuted the woman which brought forth the man child. And to the woman were given two wings of a great eagle, that she might fly into the wilderness, into her place, where she is nourished for a time, and times, and half a time, from the face of the serpent.

The symbol of the woman is derived from Genesis 37:10: "*And he told it to his father, and to his brethren: and his father rebuked him, and said unto him, What is this dream that thou hast dreamed? Shall I and thy mother and thy brethren indeed come to bow down ourselves to thee to the earth?*"

Joseph told his father, Jacob, of a dream he'd had, that the sun, moon, and eleven stars will bow down before him. Jacob then tries to clarify the meaning of the sun, moon, and stars when he questioned Joseph as to whether Jacob, Joseph's mother, and Joseph's brothers indeed would come to bow down to the earth before him.

In Genesis 35:10, Jacob's name was changed to Israel: "*And God said unto him, Thy name is Jacob: thy name shall not be called any more Jacob, but Israel shall be thy name: and he called his name Israel.*"

Jacob (Israel) fathered the nation of Israel. Joseph provides a vision of the future of the nation of Israel, when the Lord Jesus will reign from the city of Jerusalem, and the nation of Israel—along with all nations of the world—will indeed bow before him.

Based on my understanding, I cannot say with any certainty who the man child is in Revelation 12:5; however, I cannot accept the conventional teaching that the man child is the Lord Jesus.

My candidates for the man child are the 144,000 evangelist of Revelation 7:1-8, or the midtribulation saints that receive Christ as their savior during the first half of the tribulation period, or both. They may very well be caught up to God's throne just before the serpent is cast down to the earth, thus escaping the *Great* tribulation during the latter half of the tribulation period.

They will go on to share the same authority as was given to Jesus by God the Father. They, along with all the saints, will rule and reign over the nations with a rod of iron for a thousand years under the kingship of the Lord Jesus.

This is food for thought, because it lends support to the midtribulation view that is held by some Bible teachers and students.

I hope I have been able to clearly explain why I believe the scriptures speak of the man child as someone other than the Lord Jesus.

My **third** reason is based on the fact that the man child is caught up, and Jesus was not.

Acts 1:9-10 tells of people witnessing Jesus being taken up; he was not caught up: "*And when he had spoken these things, while they beheld, he was taken up; and a cloud received him out of their sight. And while they looked stedfastly toward heaven as he went up, behold, two men stood by them in white apparel.*"

He was not seized or snatched away in the twinkling of an eye, as is the man child in Revelation 12:5.

Only in five places in the New Testament is the word caught used with the Strong's definition (word number 726). They are Acts 8:39, 1 Thessalonians 4:17, Revelation 12:5, and 2 Corinthians 12:2 and 4.

Vine's Complete Expository Dictionary defines the word caught, or caught up, as a catching or snatching away by force. It is generally taught that the catching away of the saints at the pretribulation translation takes place in an instant, in a moment, in the twinkling of an eye.

If we take a look again at the ascension of Jesus in Acts 1:9-10, we see that he was observed while being taken up. He was not caught up by force, or in an instant, or in the twinkling of an eye: *"And when he had spoken these things, while they beheld, he was taken up; and a cloud received him out of their sight. And while they looked stedfastly toward heaven as he went up, behold, two men stood by them in white apparel."*

Now, ask yourself the following question: If Jesus was not caught up but rather was observed ascending and the man child is actually caught up or snatched up by force to God's throne, how can the man child in Revelation 12:5 be the Lord Jesus?

I hope you understand why I must therefore conclude that the man child of Revelation 12:5 is not the Lord Jesus.

Speculation on my part, strengthened by 1 Corinthians 15:22-23, allows me to consider the possibility of multiple translations of believers out of this world and to the throne of God, in accordance with God's order and timing: *"For as in Adam all die, even so in Christ shall all be made alive. But every man in his own order: Christ the firstfruits; afterward they that are Christ's at his coming."*

The *first* translation is the Lord himself in Acts 1:9. The **second** is the living church-age saints prior to the tribulation period. The **third** is the tribulation saints during the first three and a half years of Daniel's seventieth week, just before the abomination of desolation and the *Great* tribulation. The **fourth** is prior to the devil being cast down to the earth in the middle of the tribulation and is comprised of the 144,000 Jewish evangelist of Revelation 7:1-8 and 14:1-4. The **fifth** would be the two witnesses of Revelation 11. Finally, the **sixth** and last group are the tribulation saints at the end of the *Great* tribulation during the Feast of Trumpets (the Last Trump).

Like I said, this is speculation on my part; however, I see biblical evidence that would support multiple views.

If one chooses to give it further consideration, it just might help to reconcile the controversial debates over the timing of the traditionally taught rapture.

CHAPTER 5

The Comings and Gatherings of the Lord

Are they multiple and separate? Or are they the same event?

Paul's reference to the *"word of the Lord"* and the *"coming of the Lord"* in 1 Thessalonians 4:15 suggests to me that Paul was referring to the spoken words of Jesus in Matthew 24:30. Jesus spoke of a time of great trouble and of his coming and the gathering of his elect.

This coming and gathering will take place after the abomination of desolation and at the end of the tribulation period.

> *For this we say unto you by the word of the Lord, that we which are alive and remain [survive] unto the coming of the Lord shall not prevent them which are asleep.* (1 Thessalonians 4:15)

> *And then shall appear the sign of the Son of man in heaven: and then shall all the tribes of the earth mourn, and they shall see the Son of man coming in the clouds of heaven with power and great glory.* (Matthew 24:30, Jesus speaking)

The coming of Jesus in Acts 1:11 is the coming that is most spoken of by those who penned the Word of God and will take place at the end or near the end of the tribulation period: *"Which also said, Ye men of Galilee, why stand ye gazing up into heaven? this same Jesus, which is taken up from you into heaven, shall so come in like manner as ye have seen him go into heaven."*

This coming is not one that takes place in an instant or twinkling of an eye. Note that they observed Jesus being taken up, and a cloud received him out of their sight.

I want to emphasize that he was not caught up or snatched away. Jesus will be seen descending from heaven with the clouds of heaven. Every eye will see him—that means everybody—as stated in Revelation 1:7: *"Behold, he cometh with clouds; and every eye shall see him, and they also which pierced him: and all kindreds of the earth shall wail because of him. Even so, Amen."*

The apostle Paul also acknowledges the coming of the Lord and a gathering unto to him in 2 Thessalonians 2:1, 3. Paul states that the coming and gathering will not occur until after the tribulation period has begun and the Antichrist is revealed: *"Now we beseech you, brethren, by the coming of our Lord Jesus Christ, and by our gathering together unto him . . . Let no man deceive you by any means: for that day shall not come, except there come a falling away first, and that man of sin be revealed, the son of perdition."*

The term falling away as used in verse 3 is the Greek word apostasy. It is word number 646 in the Strong's Concordance and is defined as a defection from truth, not a defection from faith, as is most often taught.

When one turns from the truth, one turns to a lie. *"And with all deceivableness of unrighteousness in them that perish; because they received not the love of the truth, that they might be saved.*

And for this cause God shall send them strong delusion, that they should believe a lie" (2 Thessalonians 2:10-11).

In other words, the coming and gathering of the Lord will occur after the Antichrist makes his appearance. His appearance will take place at the beginning of the tribulation period, after the defection from truth occurs.

This defection from the truth (apostasy) is most likely to be the existing condition just prior to the departure of the church. After the church makes its departure, then the Antichrist will come upon the world scene.

In Revelation 14:14-16, the coming, reaping, and harvest gathering mentioned by the apostle John confirms a coming and gathering toward the end of the tribulation period.

At this point, I would like you to compare Revelation 14:14 to Matthew 24:30: *And I looked, and behold a white cloud, and upon the cloud one sat like unto the Son of man, having on his head a **golden crown**, and in his hand a **sharp sickle**.* (Revelation 14:14)

> *And then shall appear the sign of the Son of man in heaven: and then shall all the tribes of the earth mourn, and they shall see the Son of man coming in the clouds of heaven with **power** and **great glory**.* (Matthew 24:30)

In Revelation 14:14, mention is made of a **golden crown**; this is a symbol of glory. There is also mention of a **sharp sickle**; this is a symbol of power. In Matthew 24:30, mention is made of both **power and great glory**.

Now, it appears to me that these two verses are not two different events at two different times but rather describe the same event at a time near the end of the tribulation period.

It is my opinion that these two scriptures are describing the rapture of the tribulation saints, when the Lord comes and gathers his elect from the four corners of the earth at the Last Trump.

The last witness we will get a statement from is the Lord Jesus himself. Jesus said in Matthew 24:29-31 (paraphrased) that after the tribulation of those days, the Son of man will be seen coming on the clouds of heaven and will send out his angels to gather his elect from one end of heaven to the other.

> *Immediately after the tribulation of those days shall the sun be darkened, and the moon shall not give her light, and the stars shall fall from heaven, and the powers of the heavens shall be shaken: And then shall appear the sign of the Son of man in heaven: and then shall all the tribes of the earth mourn, and they shall see the Son of man coming in the clouds of heaven with power and great glory. And he shall send his angels with a great sound of a trumpet, and they shall gather together his elect from the four winds, from one end of heaven to the other.* (Matthew 24:29-31)

We know this gathering takes place near the end of the tribulation period, because the days of tribulation that Jesus speaks of in Matthew 24:15 follow the abomination of desolation: "*When ye therefore shall see the abomination of desolation, spoken of by Daniel the prophet, stand in the holy place, (whoso readeth, let him understand:).*" The abomination of desolation coincides with the casting down of the dragon (the devil) to earth during the middle of the tribulation period, as stated in Revelation 12:9: "*And the great dragon was cast out, that old serpent, called the Devil, and Satan, which deceiveth the whole world: he was cast out into the earth, and his angels were cast out with him.*"

So I believe Paul's mention in 1 Thessalonians 4:15, 17 of those who remain until the coming of the Lord was in reference to a coming and gathering of the elect near the end of the tribulation period, as mentioned in Matthew 24:30-31; 2 Thessalonians 2:1, 3; and Revelation 14:14, 16.

In all four of these scripture references, there is mention of a coming and a gathering. Ask yourself this question: Are these four different comings and four different gatherings, or are they the same event? If they are different, I'm really confused. If they are the same, then I can make sense of them.

CHAPTER 6

The Gap

Let us consider a concept that a seven-year gap of time exists between the pretribulation translation of the church-age saints and the tribulation saints, who survived until the coming of the Lord at the end of the tribulation period. Those tribulation believers will realize that their escape from a time of terrible persecution will finally come to pass when they are caught up to be with the Lord.

I feel confident that this seven-year gap theory would parallel a teaching by Hal Lindsey. During one of his past programs of The Hal Lindsey Report, he stated that a simple comma inserted in scripture can bridge a gap of time thousands of years in duration.

Lindsey points out that Jesus himself demonstrated a gap concept in Luke 4:18-21 when Jesus abruptly quits reading Isaiah 61 halfway through verse 2.

> *The Spirit of the Lord is upon me, because he hath anointed me to preach the gospel to the poor; he hath sent me to heal the brokenhearted, to preach deliverance to the captives, and recovering of sight to the blind, to set at liberty them that are bruised, To preach the acceptable year of the Lord. And he closed*

> *the book, and he gave it again to the minister, and sat down. And the eyes of all them that were in the synagogue were fastened on him. And he began to say unto them, This day is this scripture fulfilled in your ears.* (Luke 4:18-21)

Jesus reads Isaiah 61:2 up to the middle of the verse, *"To proclaim the acceptable year of the Lord."* Jesus quits reading at this point, but the verse continues as follows: *"and the day of vengeance of our God; to comfort all that mourn."*

After he stops reading, he tells those in the synagogue that he has just fulfilled this scripture. My understanding of why he stopped reading where he did was to fulfill prophecy to a point in time (approximately AD 28) when he proclaims the acceptable year of the Lord. The rest of the prophecy would not be fulfilled for over two thousand years, until the time comes for God to pour out his vengeance on an unbelieving world.

This same concept can be applied to 1 Thessalonians 4:16-17. I believe there will be a time gap of approximately seven years between verses 16 and 17:

> *For the Lord himself shall descend from heaven with a shout, with the voice of the archangel, and with the trump of God: and the dead in Christ shall rise first.*

[Seven-year time gap, or Daniel's seventieth week.]

> *Then we which are alive and remain shall be caught up together with them in the clouds, to meet the Lord in the air: and so shall we ever be with the Lord.*

The living believers—the dead in Christ—will rise first, before the seven-year tribulation begins. After a seven-year gap of time, the tribulation saints who survive until the coming of the Lord will then be caught up to be with the Lord at his Second Coming to the earth, at the Last Trump.

At this time, I want to present my interpretation of 1 Thessalonians 4:15-18. So hang on; it's going to be a little different.

In verse 15, Paul is reminding the Thessalonians that those who survive the tribulation period will not enter the Lord's presence before all those who, throughout all the ages, have fallen asleep in Jesus: *"For this we say unto you by the word of the Lord, that we which are alive and remain unto the coming of the Lord shall not prevent them which are asleep."*

Paul then goes on to say in verse 16 that the Lord will descend to the earth at the end of the tribulation period, at the Last Trump, just as Jesus said in Matthew 24:30-32.

But before Paul continues with verse 17, as if it were an afterthought, he pauses midverse to let the Thessalonians know that before the tribulation starts, the living believers—those who are alive and in Christ—will be translated into the presence of the Lord.

Then Paul continues with verse 17, stating that the tribulation saints will be caught up in spirit at the Last Trump. It is at this time that they join the multitudes who are already in the presence of the Lord.

Well, I told you it would be different. I sure hope it made some sort of sense.

Chapter 7

What's in a Cloud?

This may sound ridiculous, but do you think the Lord Jesus needs an accumulation of water vapor (which makes up an atmospheric cloud) as a mode of transportation? In several scriptures, Jesus is described as having a fluff of this stuff around and about him.

Do we really want to accept the concept that when a cloud is mentioned, it always refers to an atmospheric cloud? Or shall we consider the possibility that in several passages the word cloud may have been used to describe something other than an atmospheric cloud?

Let's look at the epistle to the Hebrews, chapter 11, also known as the faith chapter. This chapter contains a list of patriarchs and the faith attributed to them.

We don't know the exact number, but I think we could safely say it would include a great number of those who walked by faith. The reason I feel safe in saying it was a great number is because the author of Hebrews said it first. Hebrews 12:1 states, *"Wherefore seeing we also are compassed about with so great a cloud of witnesses."*

Notice he said a *"cloud of witnesses."* Now, what do you think he meant when he used the word cloud? Do you think he meant an accumulation of water vapor that makes up an atmospheric cloud? Or could it be that he was trying to express to us what a multitude of witnesses would resemble when gathered together?

Take a few seconds and imagine a massive crowd of people coming over the crest of a hill at a distance. Would they not give the appearance of a cloud rolling over the top of the hill and down into a valley?

A cloud is also referenced in Acts 1:9, when Jesus was taken up: *"And when he had spoken these things, while they beheld, he was taken up; and a **cloud** received him out of their sight."* Now, do we want to accept this cloud to be an atmospheric cloud, or could it be descriptive of something other than water vapor?

Since the day of Pentecost had not arrived as of yet to those who witnessed the ascension of Jesus, I'm inclined to believe that the cloud that received Jesus out of their sight may have been either a multitude of Old Testament saints, a host of angels, or both. And being a multitude so great in number, its appearance was that of a cloud.

Jesus speaks of his coming in the clouds of heaven at the end of the tribulation in Matthew 24:30: *"And then shall appear the sign of the Son of man in heaven: and then shall all the tribes of the earth mourn, and they shall see the Son of man coming in the **clouds** of heaven with power and great glory."*

When the day of the Lord comes to an end, I am certain there will be a mighty throng of church-age saints along with a multitude of Old Testament saints and holy angels. They will come with Jesus when he comes to gather his elect, his tribulation saints.

In verse 30 above, the word clouds (plural) is used by Jesus to describe, in part, his Second Coming. This event will take place at the end of the tribulation period during the Feast of Trumpets, or the Last Trump.

There are two groups of saints in heaven when Jesus returns: the Old Testament saints, and the Church-age saints.

In Matthew 24:30, Jesus said he is coming in the clouds with power and great glory. In Matthew 25:31, Jesus explains that when the Son of man comes, the holy angels (two thirds of his created angels) will come with him. Then he will sit upon the throne of his glory, the throne of David: "*When the Son of man shall come in his glory, and all the holy angels with him, then shall he sit upon the throne of his glory.*"

Knowing that there are two groups of saints in heaven, we can now add a third group to the list. The third group would be the holy angels. That makes three groups representing the clouds of heaven, and they will come with Jesus when he returns.

I personally have concluded that the clouds of heaven spoken of by Jesus and the apostle Paul are representative at one time or another of the multitudes of holy angels and the Old and New Testament saints.

CHAPTER 8

Why Meet the Lord in the Atmosphere?

The apostle Paul said in 1 Thessalonians 4:17 that those who remain will meet the Lord in the air: "*Then we which are alive and remain shall be caught up together with them in the clouds, to* <u>*meet*</u> *the Lord in the air: and so shall we ever be with the Lord.*" I find it very difficult to accept that the Lord would want to have a meeting in the atmosphere.

I will now make an attempt to demonstrate that the meeting in the air in verse 17 will not take place in the atmosphere as generally taught. My interpretation may have or may not have some validity; if nothing else, it's food for thought.

Let's start by zeroing in on three questions regarding the church's disappearance. First, when did it disappear? Second, how fast did it disappear? Third, and most important, where did it disappear to?

We don't have to look very far to find answers. The answers to these three questions are found in Revelation 4:1-2: "*After this I looked, and, behold, a door was opened in heaven: and the first voice which I heard was as it were of a trumpet talking with me; which said, Come up hither, and I will shew thee things which must be hereafter. And immediately I was in the spirit: and, behold, a throne was set in heaven, and one sat on the throne.*"

Question One: When Does the Church Disappear?

In Revelation 4:1-2, John's explanation of the rapture of the church—the pretribulation translation—is generally taught by many Bible teachers to be representative of the immediate translation from a physical realm to the spiritual realm.

Chapters 4 and 5 provide a description of what the apostle John saw while he was in the spirit before the throne of God. Keep in mind that everything from this point on that John is shown is in John's future.

In Revelation 6:2, Jesus opens the first seal judgment. Then the Antichrist is described making his appearance riding on a white horse (symbolizing peace), wearing a crown (symbolizing authority), and carrying a bow (symbolizing his intent to conquer): *"And I saw, and behold a white horse: and he that sat on him had a bow; and a crown was given unto him: and he went forth conquering, and to conquer."*

Because the church in Revelation is no longer mentioned after Revelation 4:1-2, it implies that the church, the body of Christ, is nowhere to be found on earth until Revelation 19:14: *"And the armies which were in heaven followed him upon white horses, clothed in fine linen, white and clean."* Keep in mind that the armies of heaven include the Old and New Testament saints and the holy angels.

I demonstrated in chapter 5 of this book ("The Comings and Gatherings of the Lord") that the restrainer, the indwelling Holy Spirit, is taken out of the way at the end of the church age.

When he is taken out of the way, the church-age saints—the body of Christ—are taken out with him. Then, and only then, will the Antichrist make his appearance.

Knowing the Antichrist makes his appearance in Revelation 6:2, I must conclude that the church-age saints have been translated to heaven before the Antichrist makes his appearance.

The church is not seen again on the earth until Revelation 19:14, when the Lord Jesus returns from his throne in heaven. He will bring the armies of heaven (the angels and saints) with him. It's at this time the Lord will battle the nations and put an end to the tribulation.

We know that the church is on earth in chapter 3, and we know the church is missing before chapter 6. John describes in Revelation 4:5 the activity going on in heaven. It appears that the church is in heaven and is involved in those activities.

To answer my *first question* as to when the church (the body of Christ) disappears, I believe that Revelation 4:1-2 best represent the time of the pretribulation translation of the church-age saints. This teaching is commonly taught by many Bible commentators and teachers.

Question Two: How Fast Does the Church Disappear?

In Revelation 4:1-2, John was given the command to "*come up hither.*" John said he was immediately in the spirit: "*After this I looked, and, behold, a door was opened in heaven: and the first voice which I heard was as it were of a trumpet talking with me; which said, Come up hither, and I will shew thee things which must be hereafter. And **immediately** I was in the spirit: and, behold, a throne was set in heaven, and one sat on the throne.*"

The Random House College Dictionary, Revised Edition, defines the word immediately to be: "*without laps of time; without delay; instantly; at once.*"

This brings to mind what the apostle Paul said in 1 Corinthians 15:51-52, regarding the tribulation saints: *"Behold, I shew you a mystery; We shall not all sleep, but we shall all be changed, In a moment, in the twinkling of an eye, at the last trump: for the trumpet shall sound, and the dead shall be raised incorruptible, and we shall be changed."* We shall all change in a moment, in the twinkling of an eye, at the Last Trump? Wow, a twinkling of an eye—now that's super fast.

Paul also implies in 2 Corinthians 5:6, 8 that as long as we are alive we are not with the Lord: *"Therefore we are always confident, knowing that, whilst we are at home in the body, we are absent from the Lord . . . we are confident, I say, and willing rather to be absent from the body, and to be present with the Lord."*

However, through trust in the Lord we can have the confidence that when we die our spirit goes, directly and without delay, into the presence of the Lord—and that's a good thing.

Hopefully, this should answer the second question as to how fast the church in Revelation 4:2 disappears.

Question Three: Where Did the Church Disappear To?

Now to answer question three, which to me is the most important one: Where did the church disappear to?

As John stated in Revelation 4:2, he was translated immediately from a physical realm to a spiritual realm: *"And **immediately** I was in the spirit: and, behold, a **throne** was set in heaven, and one sat on the **throne**."*

That spiritual realm placed him squarely before the throne of God in heaven.

If this verse represents the translation of the church, then I can say with confidence that the church is translated before the Antichrist makes his appearance at the beginning of the seven-year tribulation period and that the translation takes place instantaneously.

Most importantly, the church is translated to nowhere else but before the throne of God, before the one who sits upon the throne of heaven.

If the pretribulation translation in Revelation 4:2 represents the translation of the church, we now have a problem of reconciliation.

John stated that it was an instantaneous translation while he was in the spirit and that he was taken directly to the throne of God.

How can we reconcile what John said in Revelation 4:2 and Paul's statement in 1 Thessalonians 4:17: "*Then we which are alive and remain shall be caught up together with them in the clouds, **to meet the Lord in the air**: and so shall we ever be with the Lord*"?

Paul said that when the saints are caught up they will meet the Lord in the air, not in the spirit or at the throne of God as John stated in Revelation 4:2. Do you understand the discrepancy? One destination is in the physical realm (the atmosphere), and the other is in the spiritual realm (the throne of heaven).

How do we reconcile Revelation 4:2 and 1 Thessalonians 4:17?

This is where I'm going to take some liberty and suggest to you that Paul's use of the word air may have been better translated as spirit, as John did in Revelation 4:2: "*And immediately I was in the spirit.*"

To me it is more logical and makes better sense to believe that we (the church-age saints) will meet the Lord in the spiritual realm at the pretribulation translation and be brought into his presence before his throne.

When the tribulation saints are caught up at the end of the tribulation period, they also will be caught up in the spirit and be gathered together with the church-age saints and meet the Lord in the heavens.

Now, isn't it cooler to meet the Lord in the heavens than it is to meet him way up high in the atmosphere—especially if you are afraid of heights?

CHAPTER 9

Changed at the Last Trump

When Paul in 1 Corinthians 15:51 speaks of those who are asleep, he is making reference to those saints who are physically dead and in the grave: "*Behold, I shew you a mystery; We shall not all sleep, but we shall all be changed.*"

At the end of the tribulation period, there are those saints who are physically dead (asleep in the grave) and those saints who are alive when the Lord descends to earth to gather the living believers as described in Matthew 24:31: "*And he shall send his angels with a great sound of a trumpet, and they shall gather together his elect from the four winds, from one end of heaven to the other.*"

Just as it was with the church-age saints prior to the tribulation period, the translation of the tribulation saints who survive until the coming of the Lord will take place when the Lord comes to gather his elect, as described by Jesus in Matthew 24:31.

This is the event I consider to be the true rapture (the Last Trump) as defined by the apostle Paul in 1 Corinthians 15:51-52: "*Behold, I shew you a mystery; We shall not all sleep, but we shall all be changed, In a moment, in the twinkling of an eye, at the last trump: for the trumpet shall sound, and the dead shall be raised incorruptible, and we shall be changed."*

Please note that Paul again uses the word sleep in verse 51 and uses the word dead in verse 52. Why didn't Paul use the word asleep in verse 52? Could it be that in verse 52 Paul is speaking of all the living believers who are dead to sin and are alive in Christ (the dead in Christ)?

Let us look at verse 51. Paul says, *"Behold, I shew you a mystery; We shall not all sleep, but we shall all be changed."* In other words, not all are going to be in the grave. Ask yourself, if we shall not all sleep, doesn't that imply that some shall still be alive when we are all changed? I believe it does.

Now, in verse 52 it says this change shall take place in a single instant, in the twinkling of an eye. Keep in mind that Paul is speaking of all who sleep in Jesus and those who are alive at his coming. This includes all Old Testament saints, all the church-age saints, and all the tribulation saints. They shall all, all, all be changed in the same moment, at the same instant, at the Last Trump.

Verse 52 states that only the dead saints shall be raised incorruptible. If this is true, what about the living saints at the time the Last Trump sounds? Why are only the dead raised incorruptible? Could it be that Paul is once again using the word dead to describe those who are dead to sin but alive in Christ?

I believe he is, just as he did with the church-age saints in 1 Thessalonians 4:16 when he said, *"For the Lord himself shall descend from heaven with a shout, with the voice of the archangel, and with the trump of God: and the dead in <u>Christ</u> shall rise first."*

If this is true, then the dead who are raised incorruptible will include both the living saints and the physically dead saints. And this will take place in the twinkling of an eye, simultaneously, at the Last Trump.

Paul also said that which is corruptible cannot enter the kingdom of God. Paul made that very clear in 1 Corinthians 15:50: *"Now this I say, brethren, that flesh and blood cannot inherit the kingdom of God; neither doth corruption inherit incorruption."*

I believe when the last trumpet sounds at the end of the tribulation period, the first resurrection event will occur. I believe this is the first resurrection spoken of by Daniel, in Daniel 12:1-3, and John, in Revelation 20:4-6.

> *And at that time shall Michael stand up, the great prince which standeth for the children of thy people: and there shall be a time of trouble, such as never was since there was a nation even to that same time: and at that time thy people shall be delivered, every one that shall be found written in the book. And many of them that sleep in the dust of the earth shall awake, some to everlasting life, and some to shame and everlasting contempt. And they that be wise shall shine as the brightness of the firmament; and they that turn many to righteousness as the stars for ever and ever.* (Daniel 12:1-3)

> *And I saw thrones, and they sat upon them, and judgment was given unto them: and I saw the souls of them that were beheaded for the witness of Jesus, and for the word of God, and which had not worshipped the beast, neither his image, neither had received his mark upon their foreheads, or in their hands; and they lived and reigned with Christ a thousand years. But the rest of the dead lived not again until the thousand years were finished. This is the first resurrection. Blessed and*

> *holy is he that hath part in the first resurrection: on*
> *such the second death hath no power, but they shall be*
> *priests of God and of Christ, and shall reign with him a*
> *thousand years.* (Revelation 20:4-6)

I believe this is the time when we all will receive our resurrection bodies—all at the same moment, all at the same instant, and all at the Last Trump—thus ending the dispensation of grace.

CHAPTER 10

The Last Trump: When?

I personally do not like to use the word rapture regarding the church's departure. The term rapture best describes the Lord's gathering of his tribulation saints at the end of the tribulation period. They are the ones who must survive until they are caught up at his Second Coming.

I believe in a pretribulation departure of church-age believers. I also believe they are translated directly to heaven when the Holy Spirit is taken out of the way and is no longer restraining evil. This event will make way for the Antichrist to come onto the scene at a time of God's choosing.

Everybody has his or her own concept as to when the Last Trump will occur. Well, I guess I'm one of them. So I would like to give you my take on some controversial subjects.

Date Setters

There are many Bible teachers who, for some reason or another, don't want to be considered date setters. I don't have a problem with them, if that's what they want. Personally, I don't mind being looked at as a date setter; however, if I'm ridiculed for it and branded as being foolish, then that tends to get my hackles up.

When I was in the workforce, and when the annual Feast of Trumpets would come around, I would make my coworkers aware of the possibility of the rapture taking place. They would come back at me jokingly and kid me, saying if it didn't happen they might have to stone me for being a false prophet. Of course, they were not serious . . . at least I don't think they were. Anyway, we had fun with it. It helped to stimulate conversations regarding biblical matters. It would also stimulate the curiosity of those who were not aware of Bible prophecy.

Some whom I spoke with would be serious about not setting dates for the rapture, and they would come back at me by quoting Mark 13:32: "*But of that day and that hour knoweth no man, no, not the angels which are in heaven, neither the Son, but the Father.*"

I'm not sure if they actually understood the passage of scripture they were referring to or if they were just repeating what they had been taught. To be honest with you, the passage that this verse refers to, based on its context, still has me a little uncertain as to its correct interpretation.

After having this verse thrown at me so often when bringing up the subject of the rapture, I decided to change my tactics. I chose not to speak of the rapture, but instead I would stimulate conversation regarding the start of the seven-year tribulation period.

I can't recall any scripture saying we cannot know the hour, day, week, month, or the sabbatical cycle that will start the tribulation. However, the exact year is the big question. So I began searching the scriptures for clues.

For those of you who are a little skittish about setting dates, or even considering the possibilities, let me remind you as to who the greatest date setter of all time is—that's right, it's the Lord God himself.

Go over to Leviticus chapter 23 and read the chapter for yourself. If that isn't convincing enough, go over to Daniel 9:24-27. The angel Gabriel indirectly sets the date for the first coming of the Messiah.

In 1 Corinthians 15:51-53, the apostle Paul set a date for the resurrection. He said it would happen at the Last Trump (the Feast of Trumpets) or the first day of the seventh month of Tishri. The Last Trump is the Feast of Trumpets, and it occurs on the first day of the seventh month of Tishri, according to the Jewish sacred calendar. Wow, that sure sounds like date setting to me.

For those of you who take into consideration certain feast days for the possibility of the rapture, I remind you that you are setting dates according to the Jewish sacred calendar?

Unsettled Fact

I would like to zero in on the controversy regarding the timing of the Last Trump. As a prophecy buff for over thirty years, I find this controversy still looms before us. The timing of when the Last Trump will occur is still an unsettled fact . . . or is it? I might as well add my perspective to the mix.

The command to observe the Feast of Trumpets (the Last Trump) is given in Leviticus 23:23-24: *"And the Lord spake unto Moses, saying, Speak unto the children of Israel, saying, In the seventh month, in the first day of the month, shall ye have a sabbath, a memorial of blowing of trumpets, an holy convocation."*

I'm going to take what I hope is a logical and factual approach to discerning the timing of the Last Trump. I will start with the month of Nisan.

The Month of Nisan

Let us start in Exodus 12:1-2: *"And the Lord spake unto Moses and Aaron in the land of Egypt saying, This month shall be unto you the beginning of months: it shall be the first month of the year to you."*

During the time of the exodus out of Egypt, God commands Moses and Aaron to adjust the calendar that was in use at that time. God commanded Moses and Aaron to make the present month to be the beginning of months; and to make it the first month of their new sacred calendar.

In order to know the name of the month, we need to go over to Exodus 13:3-4: *"And Moses said unto the people, Remember this day, in which ye came out from Egypt, out of the house of bondage; for by strength of hand the Lord brought you out from this place: there shall no leavened bread be eaten. This day came ye out in the month Abib."*

Moses told the people that took part in the exodus to remember the day they were brought out of slavery and from under the rule of the pharaoh of Egypt.

In Deuteronomy 16:1, where the law of the feasts is given, the people were told to observe the Passover in the month of Abib: *"Observe the month of Abib, and keep the Passover unto the Lord thy God: for in the month of Abib the Lord thy God brought thee forth out of Egypt by night."*

This was to be an annual reminder of the time God brought them out of Egypt by night. If you do a study of the Hebrew calendar, you'll find that the month of Abib is also referred to as the month of Nisan.

Two Calendars

The Jewish people have two calendars. The modern-day Jewish civil calendar starts with the month of Tishri. The religious, sacred calendar—the one God commanded Moses to use—starts with the month of Nisan.

The two calendars are offset by six months. I strongly recommend that you use the Hebrew sacred (religious) calendar when you study biblical dates. If you try to use our modern-day Gregorian calendar, you're going to get your head all messed up. This is one of the reasons why there is so much controversy regarding the days and dates of the resurrection of Jesus.

Dates on the Hebrew sacred calendar are fixed and consistent. When converted to the Gregorian calendar, the Gregorian dates float throughout the calendar and are neither fixed nor consistent.

When studying biblical dates, study them first on the Jewish sacred calendar and then convert them to the Gregorian calendar. Don't try to make biblical dates and days fit the Gregorian calendar. The days and dates on the Hebrew sacred calendar regarding the festivals of the Lord are always consistent.

Time Segment

A time segment of one year is always followed by another time segment of one year. Ever since the human race adopted a time segment of one year as a unit measure, these time segments cycles one after another consecutively. It has done so in the past, it does so in the present, and it will do so in the future.

Let's consider a number of yearly cycles that are approximately four thousand consecutive years in duration. For the sake of argument, I want to stress that the numbers of days or months in each of these annual cycles of years will not be an issue.

Let's use the time of the exodus (approximately 1450 BC) as a starting point for the four thousand yearly cycles based on the Hebrew sacred calendar. Keep in mind that each of these annual time segments were divided into a series of months.

Nisan, Sivan, Tishri

God told Moses to start a new sacred calendar and that the first month of year was to be called Abib (Nisan).

So from this point on I will refer to the month of Abib as the month of Nisan.

In each of these consecutive years, I would like you to consider three particular months. They will be the first month of *Nisan*, the third month of *Sivan*, and the seventh month of *Tishri*. Keep in mind that we should work with the Jewish sacred calendar, which begins in the month of Nisan.

Festivals of the Lord

Now, at some point, you will have to go to Leviticus 23 and study for yourself the passages from verse 1 through 44.

Verses 1-3 speak to the weekly seventh-day Sabbath, a solemn day of rest. It is to be strictly observed every Sabbath day; the seventh day of the week.

Verses 4-44 speak of what is known as the festivals of the Lord. Don't mistake these festivals for the Jewish holidays. These festivals were given to Moses and the Israelites, who were commanded by God to observe them annually.

The festivals were to be a foreshadowing of events that would take place in Israel's future. They are also known as the feasts of the Lord. They will eventually have their fulfillment in the person of Jesus of Nazareth and at God's appointed times.

As you study these feast days, you'll become aware that there are three feast days in the first month of Nisan and one in the third month of Sivan. They are known as the spring festivals: *Passover, Unleavened Bread, Firstfruits,* and *Pentecost.*

There are also three feast days in the seventh month of *Tishri.* They represent the fall festivals: *Feast of Trumpets, Day of Atonement,* and *Tabernacles.*

The Shmita Year

At this point, I want to bring your attention to Leviticus 25:1-7, the law of the Sabbath year. Let us look specifically at Leviticus 25:3-4: *"Six years thou shalt sow thy field, and six years thou shalt prune thy vineyard, and gather in the fruit thereof; but in the seventh year shall be a sabbath of rest unto the land, a sabbath for the Lord: thou shalt neither sow thy field, nor prune thy vineyard."*

This law pertains to an agricultural cycle of seven years. The last year of this seven-year sabbatical cycle is called a *Shmita* year. It is the year when the land shall lie at rest and is forbidden to be worked.

Daniel's Seventieth Week

I want us to look at a Shmita year in light of Daniel's prophecy of seventy weeks.

In Daniel 9:20-23, Daniel was in prayer when the angel Gabriel appeared to him. In Daniel 9:24-27, Gabriel revealed to Daniel that God would bring about a certain number of events that would occur over a period of 490 years.

Gabriel referred to this 490-year time period as seventy weeks. A week of years is equivalent to seven years.

Dividing 490 years by a week of seven years, you end up with seventy weeks of years: 490 / 7 = 70.

> *Seventy weeks are determined upon thy people and upon thy holy city, to finish the transgression, and to make an end of sins, and to make reconciliation for iniquity, and to bring in everlasting righteousness, and to seal up the vision and prophecy, and to anoint the most Holy. Know therefore and understand, that from the going forth of the commandment to restore and to build Jerusalem unto the Messiah the Prince shall be seven weeks, and threescore and two weeks: the street shall be built again, and the wall, even in troublous times. And after threescore and two weeks shall Messiah be cut off, but not for himself: and the people of the prince that shall come shall destroy the city and the sanctuary; and the end thereof shall be with a flood, and unto the end of the war desolations are determined. And he shall confirm the covenant with many for one week: and in the midst of the week he shall cause the sacrifice and the oblation to cease, and for the overspreading of abominations he shall make it desolate, even until the consummation, and that determined shall be poured upon the desolate. (Daniel 9:24-27)*

In verse 25, Gabriel tells us when the seventy weeks will start. They are generally thought to start when King Artaxerxes gives Nehemiah the command to rebuild Jerusalem.

In verses 25 and 26, it turns out that after sixty-nine weeks (483 years), the Messiah, Jesus, will be cut off or crucified. It is at this time, in AD 32, that the prophecy was put on hold. It has been on hold for 1982 years.

After God's dealing with the nation of Israel for sixty-nine weeks (483 years), and as of the year 2014, there still remains one more week of seven years to complete the prophecy that is yet in the future.

In verse 27, we are told that the last week of years shall be one of tribulation. Of course, the big question is when will it start?

Start of the Seventieth Week

If you go to Nehemiah 2:1-8, you will find that Nehemiah was given the command (permission and authority) to go and rebuild the walls of Jerusalem. It tells us that this occurred in the twentieth year of King Artaxerxes's reign.

According to the time line in the introduction to the book of Nehemiah in the NKJV Open Bible, the twentieth year of Artaxerxes's reign was approximately 444 BC.

The Month of Nisan

Nehemiah 2:1 not only tells us the year but also the month that the command was given. That month is the month of Nisan: *"And it came to pass in the month Nisan, in the twentieth year of Artaxerxes the king, that wine was before him: and I took up the wine, and gave it unto the king. Now I had not been beforetime sad in his presence."* We would be hard-pressed to deny these dates.

Facts

If I were to bring this to a logical conclusion based on my understanding, I would have to conclude the following:

1. In Exodus 12:1-2 God established the Jewish sacred calendar, and it starts in the month of Nisan.

2. The Jews have two calendars: one civil and one sacred. For study purposes, the sacred calendar should be used.

3. Annual time segments cycle consecutively throughout history.

4. The feasts of the Lord, as detailed in Leviticus 23:4-44, are to be observed (rehearsed) annually until the time of their actual fulfillment in the Messiah.

5. Leviticus 25:1-4 establishes the seven-year sabbatical cycle and the Shmita (seventh) year.

6. In Daniel 9:24-27 the angel Gabriel prophesied, indirectly, that starting in the first month of Nisan, seventy sabbatical cycles of seven years each were to be accomplished when dealing with the Israelites, as he stated in verse 24.

7. Each consecutive year starts in the month of Nisan, and every sabbatical cycle will also start in the month of Nisan.

8. Sixty-nine weeks of sabbatical cycles were completed at the cutting off (crucifixion) of the Messiah.

9. One more week (sabbatical cycle), starting in the month of Nisan, is still on hold and is yet to be completed.

10. It will take one more week of years of God dealing with the nation of Israel in order for God to fulfill Daniel 9:24. God will then confirm the Davidic covenant and set up the throne of David, placing his son, Yeshua, upon his holy hill in Jerusalem.

Based on these facts, my own conclusion is that the start of Daniel's seventieth week, the seven-year tribulation period, will begin in a month of Nisan based on the Jewish sacred calendar.

What Day?

As I covered before, each of the seven years during the tribulation period will begin on the first day of the first month of Nisan. Each of these years will have a seventh month beginning on the first day of the seventh month of Tishri.

Throughout Jewish history it has been taught that the feasts of the Lord were to be observed or rehearsed annually until each of them was fulfilled according to God's appointed times.

In the year AD 32, the first three feasts were fulfilled by Jesus on *Passover, Unleavened Bread*, and *First Fruits*.

The fourth was filled by God the Father and with the Holy Spirit on *Pentecost*.

The last three feasts yet to be fulfilled are the *Feast of Trumpets, Day of Atonement*, and *Tabernacles*.

The Feast of Trumpets is in the seventh year of Daniel's seventieth week (the tribulation period) on the first day of the month of Tishri. I believe this to be the last Feast of Trumpets according to God's appointed time, thus ending the age of grace.

This is when Jesus comes to gather his tribulation saints and they are caught up to meet the Lord. I believe this is the time the apostle Paul spoke of in 1 Corinthians 15:51-52: *"Behold, I shew you a mystery; We shall not all sleep, but we shall all be changed, in a moment, in the twinkling of an eye, at the **last trump**: for the trumpet shall sound, and the dead shall be raised incorruptible, and we shall be changed."*

I believe this is the day that ends the dispensation of grace; it is also the day of the first resurrection when all believers throughout all dispensations receive their glorified bodies.

From the time I first started studying the Bible, I became aware of several unresolved and controversial topics of discussion and debate. I feel these issues will directly affect those who are left behind after the body of Christ disappears off the face of this world.

Those who are left behind during the tribulation period and come to recognize Jesus as the Messiah are identified as tribulation saints.

CHAPTER 11

The Covenant

One day while having time on my hands, I began to surf the internet. I came across one of many video presentations by Chuck Missler; a bible scholar held in high regard in the biblical and prophetic community. His presentation was titled, 'How We Got Our Bible'—Session 1.

My own personal study of Daniel 9:24-27 led me to compare a Hebrew/English Transliterated Bible to the English translation of the King James Version. In my opinion, the slight variations between the two translations are not significant enough to change the meaning of the passage.

Most English translations such as the King James Version; lead us to believe that in verse twenty seven, a certain person will have the authority to confirm or strengthen a covenant with many for one week of years: (Daniel 9:24, 27) (KJV)

> *24 Seventy weeks are determined upon thy people and upon thy holy city, to finish the transgression, and to make an end of sins, and to make reconciliation for iniquity, and to bring in everlasting righteousness, and to seal up the vision and prophecy, and to anoint the most Holy.*

> *25 Know therefore and understand, that from the going forth of the commandment to restore and to build Jerusalem unto the Messiah the Prince shall be seven weeks, and threescore and two weeks: the street shall be built again, and the wall, even in troublous times.*
>
> *26 And after threescore and two weeks shall Messiah be cut off, but not for himself: and the people of the prince that shall come shall destroy the city and the sanctuary; and the end thereof shall be with a flood, and unto the end of the war desolations are determined.*
>
> *27 And he shall confirm the covenant with many for one week: and in the midst of the week he shall cause the sacrifice and the oblation to cease, and for the overspreading of abominations he shall make it desolate, even until the consummation, and that determined shall be poured upon the desolate.*

In regards to Daniel 9:27 in the KJV, no one has yet identified to my satisfaction the *covenant* that the supposed antichrist will confirm. Nor has anyone determined who the *many* are. I see no evidence of an antichrist in this passage.

While Chuck Missler was commenting on the Greek language, he said emphatically, "Greek is very, very precise." For some reason this quote stuck in the back of my mind. After once again hearing him allude to the Septuagint as being incredibly accurate, I decided to look up Daniel 9:27 in several translations of the Septuagint.

I came across one translation of the Septuagint that grabbed my attention. I bring it to your attention because it just might spark your interest.

After giving it my consideration, this translation gave me a better understanding of what I think the angel Gabriel was trying to get across to Daniel; and to those of us in this present age.

Following is the Septuagint translation of Daniel 9:24-27. Please give special attention to verse twenty seven.

SEPTUAGINT-ENGLISH
SIR LANCELOT C.L. BRENTON
Originally published by Samuel Bagster & Sons, Ltd., London 1851

24 Seventy weeks have been determined upon thy people, and upon the holy city, for sin to be ended, and to seal up transgressions, and to blot out the iniquities, and to make atonement for iniquities, and to bring in everlasting righteousness, and to seal the vision and the prophet, and to anoint the Most Holy.

25 And thou shalt know and understand, that from the going forth of the command for the answer and for the building of Jerusalem until Christ the prince there shall be seven weeks, and sixty-two weeks; and then the time shall return, and the street shall be built, and the wall, and the times shall be exhausted.

26 And after the sixty-two weeks, the anointed one shall be destroyed, and there is no judgment in him: and he shall destroy the city and the sanctuary with the prince that is coming: they shall be cut off with a flood, and to the end of the war which is rapidly completed he shall appoint the city to desolations.

27 And one week shall establish the covenant with many: and in the midst of the week my sacrifice and drink-offering shall be taken away: and on the temple

shall be the abomination of desolations; and at the
end of time an end shall be put to the desolation.

NOTE: In Luke 21:5, 6: Jesus prophesied that the temple
(sanctuary) will be torn down; and that not one stone will be left
upon the other: (Luke 21:5-6)

> *"And as some spake of the temple, how it was adorned*
> *with goodly stones and gifts, he said,*
> *As for these things which ye behold, the days will come,*
> *in the which there shall not be left one stone upon*
> *another, that shall not be thrown down."*

Jesus will see to it that his prophecy will be fulfilled. I believe it is
he (Jesus) that will orchestrate the destruction of the city and the
sanctuary in a manner and time of his choosing.

Who could Jesus possibly use to fulfill this prophecy? My
candidate of choice would be Titus; the Roman prince. He will
come on the scene after the ascension of Jesus; sometime around
the years AD 66 to AD 70.

Daniel 9:27 of the Septuagint is the verse that caught my
attention: *"And one week shall establish the covenant with many:"*

It makes no mention of any antichrist signing any covenant with
anybody. However it does say that it will take one more week, of
seven years, to establish *The Covenant.*

I am of the opinion that it is making reference to the Davidic
Covenant promised to King David in 2 Samuel 7:16-17: *"And
thine house and thy kingdom shall be established for ever before
thee: thy throne shall be established for ever. According to all these
words, and according to al this vision, so did Nathan speak unto
David."*

At this present time, the throne of David is not physically in existence in Jerusalem. The Davidic Covenant and throne will be established when Jesus returns at the end of Daniels seventieth week; but not before the son of perdition sets up the abomination of desolation in the middle of that same week; and for the last three and a half years of the week, the Lawless one will bring about great tribulation spoken of by Jesus in Matthew 24:15-30.

I think this translation is more fitting and makes more sense; while at the same time removing any controversy as to the true covenant mentioned in Daniel 9:27.

Here is where I'm going to present to you my understanding of Daniel 9:24-27; with the emphasis being on verse twenty six and twenty seven.

I have made some underlined insertions in parentheses only to present to you my understanding of what the scriptures reveal to me. Please know that my intention is not to add or take away anything from the original scriptures.

SEPTUAGINT ENGLISH
SIR LANCELOT C.L. BRENTON

Originally published by Samuel Bagster & Sons, Ltd., London 1851

Daniel 9:24-27

> 24 Seventy weeks have been determined upon thy people, and upon the holy city, for sin to be ended, and to seal up transgressions, and to blot out the iniquities, and to make atonement for iniquities, and to bring in everlasting righteousness, and to seal the vision and the prophet, and to anoint the Most Holy.

25 And thou shalt know and understand, that from the going forth (<u>in a month of Nisan</u>) of the command for the answer and for the building of Jerusalem until Christ (<u>Jesus</u>) the prince there shall be seven weeks, and sixty-two weeks; and then the time shall return, and the street shall be built, and the wall, and the times shall be exhausted.

26 And after the sixty-two weeks, the anointed one (Jesus) shall be destroyed (<u>crucified</u>), and there is no judgment in him: and he (Jesus) shall destroy the city and the sanctuary (<u>in AD 70</u>) with the (<u>Roman</u>) prince (<u>Titus</u>) that is coming (<u>in AD 66-70</u>): (<u>at that time</u>) they (<u>in Jerusalem</u>) shall be cut off with a flood, and to the end of the war (<u>the siege of Jerusalem</u>) which is rapidly completed he (Jesus) shall appoint the city to desolations (<u>for 1878 years</u>).

27 And one (<u>more</u>) week shall (<u>then</u>) establish the (<u>Davidic</u>) covenant with many (<u>peoples, tongues, and nations</u>): and in the midst of the week my sacrifice and drink-offering shall be taken away (<u>by the son of perdition</u>): and on the temple shall be the abomination of desolations; and at the end of time (<u>the end of the tribulation Period</u>) an end shall be put to the desolation.

After Jesus stomps all over the son of perdition, an angel will bind the devil with a chain; and then toss his bottom into the bottomless pit; Revalation 20:1-3 (KJV)

> "And *I saw an angel come down from heaven, having the key of the bottomless pit and a great chain in his hand. And he laid hold on the dragon, that old serpent, which is the Devil, and Satan, and bound him a thousand years, And cast him into the bottomless*

pit, and shut him up, and set a seal upon him, that he should deceive the nations no more, till the thousand years should be fulfilled: and after that he must be loosed a little season."

After the devil is cast into the bottomless pit, God will then establish the Davidic Kingdom on his Holy Hill in Jerusalem.

Jesus, the anointed one, will rule and rain upon the throne of David for a thousand years; and then forever and forever; Amen (cool).

Conclusion

Well, I hope I gave you some food for thought. I'm not saying that I hold the answers to all of these controversial topics; I'm just hoping that what I have presented to you may in some way persuade you to consider the plight of the tribulation saints by putting yourself in their shoes. Interpreting scriptures from their perspective might give us cause to change our way of thinking. Who knows . . . maybe it will change our point of view regarding some of these end-time matters.

On a Personal Note

For those who have not yet received or understood God's gift of eternal life, I want to give you some very important information that you should know. After you have read it, I want to ask you a very, very important question.

FYI

God loves you and respects you enough to honor your decision regarding your eternal destiny. If you choose to live your life without God or his precious gift of eternal life, God will honor your decision.

However, let me make something very clear so you won't have any misunderstandings about the consequence of your choice. If you don't want God in your life, you want him to leave you alone, or you want nothing to do with him, consider the following:

If you die rejecting his offer of eternal life, your eternal destiny will be sealed forever.

The choice you make in this life, he will honor in the next. He will do as you wanted and leave you alone forever. You will spend eternity apart from God in eternal despair, eternal hopelessness, and eternal regret.

Please, please understand, there will be no second chance.

You must choose between eternal life (forever in the presence of God) and eternal death (forever separated from the presence of God). You must choose today; there may be no tomorrow.

Eternal life is a gift from God. Gifts can only be received or rejected; they cannot be earned. A wage is earned based on work you perform. A gift is the result of work performed by someone else. The Word of God says we are not given the gift of eternal life based upon any works or good deeds that we might have performed.

A loving, righteous, and judging God will not allow you or me to stand before him at the judgment and, in a prideful and boastful way, say to God, "I earned my salvation, and it was based on my own good works and deeds. I didn't feel I had to follow your plan for my eternal salvation."

The sad reality of this kind of thinking and reasoning is it will keep you separated from God and his eternal kingdom forever, and forever, and forever.

God's Word says we are given the gift of eternal life when we choose to trust in the one who performed the work of salvation, the one who purchased—for you, me, and for any and all who would receive it—the gift of eternal life.

The Word of God (the Bible) states in John 3:16:

> *"For God so loved the world,* (that's you and me) *that he gave his only begotten Son,* (Jesus, the risen Christ) *that whosoever believes* (trusts) *in him should not perish, but have eternal life."*

Eternal life is freely given to you and me, but it can be difficult to receive. You have to make a sincere choice from within your spirit (heart).

Do you want to pursue the temporary things of this world that Satan has to offer, or do you want to pursue eternal life that God freely offers you?

If you are at this crossroad, please . . . choose wisely.

My question to you is what will you do with this Jesus? Will you receive him or reject him?

Your eternal destiny depends upon your answer.